Mom Vegan Recipes

Mom Vegan Main-Course Recipes

By Helena Santorini

Sommario

Introduction

Mainly there are two different types of vegetarians, some taking their beliefs to the extreme, they also prefer to eliminate products of animal origin and are called vegans, others who prefer to consume them anyway. in both cases, however, we choose to abolish any form of meat including pork, chicken, shells, beef, game and even fish. vegetarianism as a lifestyle, in addition to respecting animals, can also bring other important benefits important to one's health such as a great reduction in the risk of diabetes and other chronic diseases. if this world intrigues you, I invite you to consult our fantastic book and go in search of your favorite dish, bon appetite.

Main Course

Grilled Marinated Eggplant and Zucchini

Ingredients

2 large Eggplants, cut lengthwise and cut in half2 large Zucchinis, cut lengthwise and cut in half

Marinade Ingredients:

6 tbsp. extra virgin olive
oilSea salt, to taste

3 tbsp. distilled white
vinegar1 tsp. pesto sauce

Marinate the vegetable with the dressing or marinade ingredients for15 to 30 min.

Grill for 4 minutes over medium heat or until the vegetable becomestender.

Grilled Bell Pepper and Broccolini

Ingredients

2 Green Bell Peppers, cut in
half10 Broccolini Florets

Marinade Ingredients:

6 tbsp. extra virgin olive

oilSea salt, to taste

3 tbsp. distilled white vinegar

1 tsp. sun-dried tomato pesto sauce

Marinate the vegetable with the dressing or marinade ingredients for15 to 30 min.

Grill for 4 minutes over medium heat or until the vegetable becomestender.

Grilled Cauliflower and Brussel Sprouts

Ingredients

10 Cauliflower florets

10 pcs. Brussel Sprouts

Marinade Ingredients:

6 tbsp. extra virgin olive oilSea salt, to taste

3 tbsp. distilled white vinegar1 tsp. mayonnaise

Marinate the vegetable with the dressing or marinade ingredients for15 to 30 min.

Grill for 4 minutes over medium heat or until the vegetable becomestender.

Grilled Corn and Crimini Mushrooms

Ingredients

2 Corns, cut lengthwise

10 Crimini Mushrooms, rinsed and drained

Marinade Ingredients:

6 tbsp. extra virgin olive
oilSea salt, to taste

3 tbsp. distilled white
vinegar 1 tsp. Dijon
mustard

Marinate the vegetable with the dressing or marinade ingredients for15 to 30 min.

Grill for 4 minutes over medium heat or until the vegetable becomestender.

Grilled Eggplant, Zucchini and Corn

Ingredients

2 large Eggplants, cut lengthwise and cut in half2 large Zucchinis, cut lengthwise and cut in half2 Corns, cut lengthwise

Marinade Ingredients:

6 tbsp. extra virgin olive oilSea salt, to taste

3 tbsp. distilled white vinegar1 tsp. mayonnaise

Marinate the vegetable with the dressing or marinade ingredients for15 to 30 min.

Grill for 4 minutes over medium heat or until the vegetable becomestender.

Grilled Zucchini and Pineapple

Ingredients

2 large zucchini , cut lengthwise into ½ inch slabs

2 large red onions, cut into ½ inch rings but don't separate intoindividual rings

1 medium Pineapple, cut into 1/2 inch slices10 Green Beans

Marinade Ingredients:

6 tbsp. extra virgin olive oilSea salt, to taste

3 tbsp. distilled white vinegar1 tsp. honey

Marinate the vegetable with the dressing or marinade ingredients for15 to 30 min.

Grill for 4 minutes over medium heat or until the vegetable becomestender.

Grilled Portobello and Eggplant

Ingredients

3 pcs. Portobello, rinsed and drained

2 pcs. Eggplant, cut lengthwise and cut in
half2 pcs. Zucchini, cut lengthwise and cut
in half6 pcs. Asparagus

Marinade Ingredients:

6 tbsp. extra virgin olive oilSea salt, to taste

3 tbsp. distilled white vinegar 1 tsp. English mustard

Marinate the vegetable with the dressing or marinade ingredients for15 to 30 min.

Grill for 4 minutes over medium heat or until the vegetable becomestender.

Grilled Asparagus and Mushrooms

Ingredients

6 pcs. Crimini mushrooms, rinsed and drained 2 pcs. Eggplant, cut lengthwise and cut in half 2 pcs. Zucchini, cut lengthwise and cut in half 6 pcs. Asparagus

Dressing Ingredients

6 tbsp. extra virgin olive oil Sea salt, to taste

3 tbsp. apple cider vinegar 1 tbsp. honey

1 tsp. Egg-free mayonnaise

Marinate the vegetable with the dressing or marinade ingredients for 15 to 30 min.

Grill for 4 minutes over medium heat or until the vegetable becomes tender.

Grilled Japanese Eggplant and Shitake Mushroom

Ingredients

Corns, cut lengthwise

2 pcs. Japanese Eggplant, cut lengthwise and cut in half3 Shitake Mushrooms, rinsed and drained

Dressing
Ingredients 6 tbsp.
olive oil

Sea salt, to taste

3 tbsp.   white   wine
vinegar 1 tsp. Egg-free
mayonnaise

Marinate the vegetable with the dressing or marinade ingredients for15 to 30 min.

Grill for 4 minutes over medium heat or until the vegetable

becomestender.

Grilled Japanese Eggplant Bell Peppers and Broccolini

Ingredients

2 Green Bell Peppers, cut in
half10 Broccolini Florets

2 pcs. Japanese Eggplant, cut lengthwise and cut in half

Dressing
Ingredients 6 tbsp.
sesame oil Sea salt,
to taste

3 tbsp. distilled white
vinegar1 tsp. mayonnaise

Marinate the vegetable with the dressing or marinade ingredients for15 to 30 min.

Grill for 4 minutes over medium heat or until the vegetable becomestender.

Grilled Cauliflower and Brussel Sprouts

Ingredients

10 Cauliflower florets

10 pcs. Brussel Sprouts

Dressing
Ingredients 6 tbsp.
sesame oil

3   tbsp.   distilled   white
vinegar1 tsp. soy sauce

1 tsp. Hoi Sin Sauce

Marinate the vegetable with the dressing or marinade ingredients for15 to 30 min.

Grill for 4 minutes over medium heat or until the vegetable becomestender.

Grilled Japanese Bell Pepper and Cauliflower Recipe with Balsamic Glaze

Ingredients

2 Yellow Bell Peppers, cut in half lengthwise 10 Cauliflower Florets

2 pcs. Japanese Eggplant, cut lengthwise and cut in half

Dressing Ingredients

6 tbsp. extra virgin olive oil Sea salt, to taste

3 tbsp. Balsamic vinegar 1 tsp. Dijon mustard

Marinate the vegetable with the dressing or marinade ingredients for 15 to 30 min.

Grill for 4 minutes over medium heat or until the vegetable

becomestender.

Grilled Broccoli and Zucchini Recipe

Ingredients

2 large Eggplants, cut lengthwise and cut in half1 large Zucchini, cut lengthwise and cut in half 5 Broccoli Florets

Marinade Ingredients:

6 tbsp. extra virgin olive oilSea salt, to taste

3 tbsp. distilled white vinegar1 tsp. mayonnaise

Marinate the vegetable with the dressing or marinade ingredients for15 to 30 min.

Grill for 4 minutes over medium heat or until the vegetable becomestender.

Grilled Eggplant and Yellow Bell Peppers

Ingredients

2 Yellow Bell Peppers, cut in
half10 Broccolini Florets

2 pcs. Eggplant, cut lengthwise and cut in half

Dressing

Ingredients 6 tbsp.
olive oil

Sea salt, to taste

3 tbsp.   white   wine
vinegar1 tsp. mustard

Marinate the vegetable with the dressing or marinade ingredients
for15 to 30 min.

Grill for 4 minutes over medium heat or until the vegetable
becomestender.

Grilled Portobello Asparagus and Pineapple

Ingredients

3 pcs. Portobello, rinsed and drained

2 pcs. Eggplant, cut lengthwise and cut in half2 pcs. Zucchini, cut lengthwise and cut in half6 pcs. Asparagus

1 medium Pineapple, cut into 1/2 inch slices10 Green Beans

Dressing Ingredients

6 tbsp. extra virgin olive oilSea salt, to taste

3 tbsp. apple cider vinegar1 tbsp. honey

1 tsp. mayonnaise

Marinate the vegetable with the dressing or marinade ingredients for15 to 30 min.

Grill for 4 minutes over medium heat or until the vegetable becomestender.

Grilled Collard Greens and Portobello Mushrooms

Ingredients

1 bunch of collard greens

5 pcs. Portobello mushrooms, rinsed and drained 10 Asparagus spears

Dressing
Ingredients 6 tbsp.
olive oil

Sea salt, to taste

3 tbsp. white wine
vinegar 1 tsp. Egg-free
mayonnaise

Marinate the vegetable with the dressing or marinade ingredients for 15 to 30 min.

Grill for 4 minutes over medium heat or until the vegetable becomes tender.

Brussel Sprouts and Endives

Ingredients

10 Cauliflower florets
10 pcs. Brussel
Sprouts 1 bunch of
endives

Dressing
Ingredients 6 tbsp.
olive oil

Sea salt, to taste

3 tbsp. white wine
vinegar 1 tsp. Egg-free
mayonnaise

Marinate the vegetable with the dressing or marinade ingredients
for15 to 30 min.

Grill for 4 minutes over medium heat or until the vegetable
becomestender.

Red Cabbage and Onion in Ranch Dressing

Ingredients

1 Red cabbage

2 large red onions, cut into ½ inch rings but don't separate intoindividual rings

2 tbsp. extra virgin olive oil2 tbsp. ranch dressing mix

Marinate the vegetable with the dressing or marinade ingredients for15 to 30 min.

Grill for 4 minutes over medium heat or until the vegetable becomestender.

Grilled Green Bean and Microgreens in Balsamic Vinaigrette

Ingredients

1 bunch of microgreens 10 Green Beans Dressing Ingredients

6 tbsp. extra virgin olive oilSea salt, to taste

3 tbsp. Balsamic vinegar1 tsp. mustard

Marinate the vegetable with the dressing or marinade ingredients for15 to 30 min.

Grill for 4 minutes over medium heat or until the vegetable becomestender.

Grilled Broccolini Asparagus and Eggplants

Ingredients

1 large Eggplants, cut lengthwise and cut in
half1 bunch of turnip greens

10 Asparagus spears

10 Broccolini Florets

Marinade Ingredients:

6 tbsp. extra virgin olive
oilSea salt, to taste

3 tbsp. distilled white
vinegar 1 tsp. Dijon
mustard

Marinate the vegetable with the dressing or marinade ingredients
for15 to 30 min.

Grill for 4 minutes over medium heat or until the vegetable becomestender.

Grilled Broccolini and Turnip Greens

Ingredients

1 bunch of turnip
greens 8 Broccolini
Florets

Dressing Ingredients 6
tbsp. sesame oil Sea
salt, to taste

3 tbsp. distilled white
vinegar 1 tsp. Egg-free
mayonnaise

Marinate the vegetable with the dressing or marinade ingredients
for 15 to 30 min.

Grill for 4 minutes over medium heat or until the vegetable
becomes tender.

Grilled Rutabaga and Mustard Greens

Ingredients

1 medium Rutabaga, peeled and cut in half lengthwise

1 large red onion, cut into ½ inch rings but don't separate intoindividual rings

1 bunch of mustard greens

Dressing
Ingredients 6 tbsp.
olive oil

Sea salt, to taste

3 tbsp. white wine
vinegar 1 tsp. English
mustard

Marinate the vegetable with the dressing or marinade ingredients for15 to 30 min.

Grill for 4 minutes over medium heat or until the vegetable

becomestender.

Grilled Green Cabbage in Apple Cider Vinaigrette

Ingredients

1 large parsnip, peeled and cut lengthwise

5 pcs. Portobello mushrooms, rinsed and drained1 Green cabbage, cut in half

Dressing Ingredients

6 tbsp. extra virgin olive oilSea salt, to taste

3 tbsp. apple cider vinegar1 tbsp. honey

1 tsp. Egg-free mayonnaise

Marinate the vegetable with the dressing or marinade ingredients for15 to 30 min.

Grill for 4 minutes over medium heat or until the vegetable becomestender.

Grilled Turnips with Broccoli

Ingredients

10 Broccoli florets

1 large turnips, peeled and cut lengthwise1 Red cabbage, cut in half

Dressing
Ingredients 6 tbsp.
olive oil

Sea salt, to taste

3 tbsp. white wine vinegar 1 tsp. Egg-free mayonnaise

Marinate the vegetable with the dressing or marinade ingredients for 15 to 30 min.

Grill for 4 minutes over medium heat or until the vegetable

becomestender.

Grilled Parsnip and Rutabaga

Ingredients

1 large parsnip, peeled and cut lengthwise

1 medium Rutabaga, peeled and cut in half lengthwise

2 large red onions, cut into ½ inch rings but don't separate intoindividual rings

Marinade Ingredients:

6 tbsp. extra virgin olive oilSea salt, to taste

3 tbsp. distilled white vinegar 1 tsp. Dijon mustard

Marinate the vegetable with the dressing or marinade ingredients for15 to 30 min.

Grill for 4 minutes over medium heat or until the vegetable becomestender.

Grilled Turnip and Beetroots

Ingredients

1 large turnip, peeled and cut lengthwise 1 large carrot, peeled and cut lengthwise

1 medium Beetroot , peeled and cut in half lengthwise

Dressing
Ingredients 6 tbsp.
sesame oil Sea salt,
to taste

3 tbsp. distilled white vinegar 1 tsp. Egg-free mayonnaise

Marinate the vegetable with the dressing or marinade ingredients for 15 to 30 min.

Grill for 4 minutes over medium heat or until the vegetable becomestender.

Grilled Carrot, Turnip and Water Chestnuts with Balsamic Glaze

Ingredients

1 large carrots, peeled and cut lengthwise 1 large turnip, peeled and cut lengthwise 1/2 cup canned water chestnuts

2 pcs. Portobello mushrooms, rinsed and drained Dressing Ingredients

6 tbsp. extra virgin olive oil Sea salt, to taste

3 tbsp. Balsamic vinegar 1 tsp. Dijon mustard

Marinate the vegetable with the dressing or marinade ingredients for 15 to 30 min.

Grill for 4 minutes over medium heat or until the vegetable

becomestender.

Grilled Water Chestnuts and Mangoes

Ingredients

1/2 cup water chestnuts

2 large mangoes, cut lengthwise and pitted
Dressing Ingredients

6 tbsp. sesame
oil Sea salt, to
taste

3 tbsp. distilled white
vinegar 1 tsp. Egg-free
mayonnaise

Marinate the vegetable with the dressing or marinade ingredients for15 to 30 min.

Grill for 4 minutes over medium heat or until the vegetable becomestender.

For the mango, grill only until you start seeing brown grill marks.

Grilled beetroots and Green Beans

Ingredients

2 beetroots, peeled and sliced lengthwise

1 medium Pineapple, cut into 1/2 inch
slices 10 Green Beans

2 large red onions, cut into ½ inch rings but don't separate
into individual rings

Dressing

Ingredients 6 tbsp.
olive oil

Sea salt, to taste

3 tbsp.   white   wine
vinegar 1   tsp.   English
mustard

Marinate the vegetable with the dressing or marinade ingredients for 15 to 30 min.

Grill for 4 minutes over medium heat or until the vegetable becomestender.

Grilled Artichoke Hearts and Water Chestnuts

Ingredients

½ cup canned artichoke hearts 1/2 cup water chestnuts

10 pcs. Brussel Sprouts

Dressing
Ingredients 6 tbsp.
olive oil

Sea salt, to taste

3 tbsp. white wine vinegar 1 tsp. Egg-free mayonnaise

Marinate the vegetable with the dressing or marinade ingredients for 15 to 30 min.

Grill for 4 minutes over medium heat or until the vegetable becomestender.

Grilles Turnips Broccolini and Water Chestnuts with Honey Apple Cider Glaze

Ingredients

10 Broccolini Florets

1/2 cup water chestnuts

1 large turnip, peeled and cut lengthwise

Dressing Ingredients

6 tbsp. extra virgin olive oilSea salt, to taste

3 tbsp. apple cider vinegar1 tbsp. honey

1 tsp. Egg-free mayonnaise

Marinate the vegetable with the dressing or marinade ingredients for15 to 30 min.

Grill for 4 minutes over medium heat or until the vegetable

becomestender.

Grilled Assorted Bell Peppers with Broccolini Florets Recipe

Ingredients

1 Green Bell Pepper, cut in half

2 beetroots, peeled and sliced lengthwise1 Red Bell Pepper, cut in half

10 Broccolini Florets

Marinade Ingredients:

6 tbsp. extra virgin olive oilSea salt, to taste

3 tbsp. distilled white vinegar 1 tsp. Dijon mustard

Marinate the vegetable with the dressing or marinade ingredients for15 to 30 min.

Grill for 4 minutes over medium heat or until the vegetable becomestender.

Grilled Eggplant & Beetroot with Assorted Bell Peppers

Ingredients

1 small Eggplant, cut lengthwise and cut in half2 beetroots, peeled and sliced lengthwise

1 large turnip, peeled and cut lengthwise1 Yellow Bell Pepper, cut in half

1 Red Bell Pepper, cut in half

Dressing
Ingredients 6 tbsp.
sesame oil Sea salt,
to taste

3 tbsp. distilled white vinegar 1 tsp. Egg-free mayonnaise

Marinate the vegetable with the dressing or marinade ingredients for15 to 30 min.

Grill for 4 minutes over medium heat or until the vegetable becomestender.

Grilled Portobello and Rutabaga

Ingredients

1 medium Rutabaga, peeled and cut in half lengthwise5 pcs. Portobello mushrooms, rinsed and drained

1 medium red onion, cut into ½ inch rings but don't separate intoindividual rings

Dressing Ingredients

6 tbsp. extra virgin olive oilSea salt, to taste

3 tbsp. Balsamic vinegar 1 tsp. Dijon mustard

Marinate the vegetable with the dressing or marinade ingredients for15 to 30 min.

Grill for 4 minutes over medium heat or until the vegetable

becomestender.

Grilled Water Chestnuts Zucchini and Endives

Ingredients

2 large zucchini , cut lengthwise into ½ inch
slabs 1/2 cup water chestnuts

1 bunch of endives
Dressing
Ingredients 6 tbsp.
sesame oil Sea salt,
to taste

3 tbsp. distilled white
vinegar 1 tsp. Egg-free
mayonnaise

Marinate the vegetable with the dressing or marinade ingredients
for 15 to 30 min.

Grill for 4 minutes over medium heat or until the vegetable
becomes tender.

Grilled Brussel Sprouts Cauliflower and Rutabaga

Ingredients

1 medium Rutabaga, peeled and cut in half lengthwise 10 Cauliflower florets

5 pcs. Brussel Sprouts

1 bunch of collard greens

Dressing Ingredients 6 tbsp. olive oil

Sea salt, to taste

3 tbsp. white wine vinegar 1 tsp. English mustard

Marinate the vegetable with the dressing or marinade ingredients for 15 to 30 min.

Grill for 4 minutes over medium heat or until the vegetable becomes tender.

Grilled Collard Greens Portobello and Asparagus

Ingredients

3 pcs. Portobello, rinsed and drained

1 medium Rutabaga, peeled and cut in half lengthwise1 bunch of collard greens

6 pcs. Asparagus

Dressing

Ingredients 6 tbsp.
sesame oil Sea salt,
to taste

3 tbsp. distilled white
vinegar 1 tsp. Egg-free
mayonnaise

Marinate the vegetable with the dressing or marinade ingredients for 15 to 30 min.

Grill for 4 minutes over medium heat or until the vegetable becomes tender.

Grilled Water Chestnuts Swiss Chard and Asparagus Recipe

Ingredients

1/2 cup water chestnuts 1 bunch of swiss chard 6 pcs. Asparagus

Dressing Ingredients

6 tbsp. extra virgin olive oilSea salt, to taste

3 tbsp. apple cider vinegar1 tbsp. honey

1 tsp. Egg-free mayonnaise

Marinate the vegetable with the dressing or marinade ingredients for15 to 30 min.

Grill for 4 minutes over medium heat or until the vegetable becomestender.

Grilled Ruttabaga and Swiss Chard

Ingredients

1 medium Rutabaga, peeled and cut in half lengthwise

2 large red onions, cut into ½ inch rings but don't separate intoindividual rings

1 bunch of swiss chard

Marinade Ingredients:

6 tbsp. extra virgin olive
oilSea salt, to taste

3 tbsp. distilled white
vinegar 1 tsp. Dijon
mustard

Marinate the vegetable with the dressing or marinade ingredients for15 to 30 min.

Grill for 4 minutes over medium heat or until the vegetable becomestender.

Grilled Asparagus Pineapple and Green Beans

Ingredients

1 medium Rutabaga, peeled and cut in half lengthwise 10 pcs. Asparagus

1 medium Pineapple, cut into 1/2 inch slices 1 bunch of collard greens

Dressing
Ingredients 6 tbsp.
sesame oil Sea salt,
to taste

3 tbsp. distilled white vinegar 1 tsp. Egg-free mayonnaise

Marinate the vegetable with the dressing or marinade ingredients for 15 to 30 min.

Grill for 4 minutes over medium heat or until the vegetable becomes tender.

Grilled Green Beans and Eggplants

Ingredients

2 beetroots, peeled and sliced lengthwise

3 large Zucchinis, cut lengthwise and cut in
  half10 Green Beans

4 Dressing Ingredients

6 tbsp. extra virgin olive
oilSea salt, to taste

3   tbsp.   Balsamic
vinegar 1 tsp. Dijon
mustard

Marinate the vegetable with the dressing or marinade ingredients for15 to 30 min.

Grill for 4 minutes over medium heat or until the vegetable becomestender.

Grilled Asparagus and Broccolini

Ingredients

1 bunch of swiss chard

5 pcs. Portobello mushrooms, rinsed and drained8 pcs. Asparagus

Dressing
Ingredients 6 tbsp.
sesame oil Sea salt,
to taste

3 tbsp. distilled white
vinegar 1 tsp. Egg-free
mayonnaise

Marinate the vegetable with the dressing or marinade ingredients for15 to 30 min.

Grill for 4 minutes over medium heat or until the vegetable becomestender.

Grilled Collard Greens and Brussel Sprouts

Ingredients

1 bunch of collard greens 10 pcs. Brussel Sprouts 10 Broccolini Florets

1 bunch of swiss chard

Dressing Ingredients 6 tbsp. olive oil

Sea salt, to taste

3 tbsp. white wine vinegar 1 tsp. English mustard

Marinate the vegetable with the dressing or marinade ingredients for15 to 30 min.

Grill for 4 minutes over medium heat or until the vegetable becomestender.

Grilled Broccoli & Swiss Chard

Ingredients

2 Green Bell Peppers, cut in half1 bunch of swiss chard

5 Broccoli Florets

Dressing
Ingredients 6 tbsp.
sesame oil Sea salt,
to taste

3 tbsp. distilled white vinegar 1 tsp. Egg-free mayonnaise

Marinate the vegetable with the dressing or marinade ingredients for15 to 30 min.

Grill for 4 minutes over medium heat or until the vegetable becomestender.

Grilled Swiss Chard and Asparagus

Ingredients

1 medium Rutabaga, peeled and cut in half lengthwise

2 large red onions, cut into ½ inch rings but don't separate intoindividual rings

1 bunch of swiss
chard 10 pcs.
Asparagus

Dressing Ingredients

6 tbsp. extra virgin olive oilSea salt, to taste

3 tbsp. apple cider vinegar1 tbsp. honey

1 tsp. Egg-free mayonnaise

Marinate the vegetable with the dressing or marinade ingredients for15 to 30 min.

Grill for 4 minutes over medium heat or until the vegetable becomestender.

Grilled Water Chestnuts and Green Beans

Ingredients

10 Broccolini Florets

10 pcs. Asparagus

1/2 cup water chestnuts 10 Green Beans

Marinade Ingredients:

6 tbsp. extra virgin olive oilSea salt, to taste

3 tbsp. distilled white vinegar 1 tsp. Dijon mustard

Marinate the vegetable with the dressing or marinade ingredients for15 to 30 min.

Grill for 4 minutes over medium heat or until the vegetable becomestender.

Grilled Endives and Edamame Beans

Ingredients

10 Edamame Beans

2 beetroots, peeled and sliced lengthwise 1 bunch of endives

Dressing
Ingredients 6 tbsp.
olive oil

Sea salt, to taste

3 tbsp. white wine
vinegar 1 tsp. Egg-free
mayonnaise

Marinate the vegetable with the dressing or marinade ingredients for 15 to 30 min.

Grill for 4 minutes over medium heat or until the vegetable

becomestender.

Grilled Turnip Greens and Okra

Ingrediens

5 pcs. Okra

1 bunch of turnip greens

2 large red onions, cut into ½ inch rings but don't separate intoindividual rings

Dressing Ingredients

6 tbsp. extra virgin olive oilSea salt, to taste

3 tbsp. Balsamic vinegar 1 tsp. Dijon mustard

Marinate the vegetable with the dressing or marinade ingredients

for15 to 30 min.

Grill for 4 minutes over medium heat or until the vegetable becomestender.

Grilled Water Chestnuts and Cabbage

Ingredients

1 Green cabbage

1/2 cup water chestnuts

2 large red onions, cut into ½ inch rings but don't separate intoindividual rings

2 tbsp. extra virgin olive oil2 tbsp. ranch dressing mix

Marinate the vegetable with the dressing or marinade ingredients for15 to 30 min.

Grill for 4 minutes over medium heat or until the vegetable becomestender.

Grilled Beetroots and Purple Cabbage

Ingredients

1 large   Parsnip,   cut
lengthwise1 Purple cabbage

2 beetroots, peeled and sliced lengthwise

2 large Zucchinis, cut lengthwise and cut in half

Dressing
Ingredients 6 tbsp.
olive oil

Sea salt, to taste

3 tbsp.   white   wine
vinegar 1   tsp. English
mustard

Marinate the vegetable with the dressing or marinade ingredients
for15 to 30 min.

Grill for 4 minutes over medium heat or until the vegetable becomestender.

Conclusion

How did you like these delicious vegetarian recipes? I hope you liked them.

at this point unfortunately we have come to the end of this fantastic vegetarian cookbook, but I will write more soon so stay up to date!

We leave you with one last tip to accentuate the benefits of a healthy and balanced diet, always combine an active lifestyle and physical activity with our delicious and healthy recipes. We send you a big hug and we will soon be back to have fun and intrigue you with our recipes. See you soon.

CPSIA information can be obtained
at www.ICGtesting.com
Printed in the USA
BVHW061013130421
604814BV00008B/1385